HOW TO LIVE LIKE
A CARIBBEAN
PIRATE

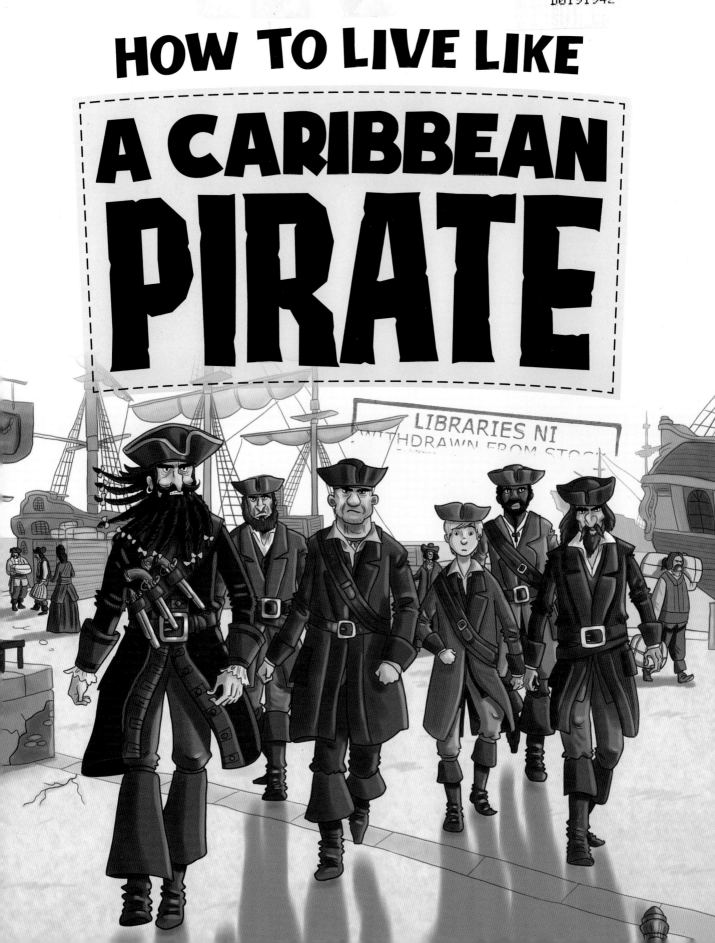

Thanks to the creative team:

Senior Editor: Alice Peebles
Consultant: John Haywood
Fack checking: Kate Mitchell

Design: www.collaborate.agency

First published in Great Britain in 2016
by Hungry Tomato Ltd
PO Box 181
Edenbridge
Kent, TN8 9DP

Copyright © 2016 Hungry Tomato Ltd.

A CIP catalogue record for this book is
available from the British Library.

ISBN 978-1-910684-42-9

Printed and bound in China

Discover more at
www.hungrytomato.com

HOW TO LIVE LIKE
A CARIBBEAN
PIRATE

by John Farndon
Illustrated by Tatio Viano

HUNGRY
TOMATO™

contents

Pirate! 6

A Pirate Ship 8

Life on Board 10

Blackbeard! 12

Walking the Plank! 14

Cutlass and Flintlock 16

Sneaky Tactics 18

Stand by to Board! 20

Booty Haul 22

Pirate Haunts 24

Dressed like a Pirate 26

That's Your Lot 28

Ten Pesky Pirate Facts 30

Glossary 31

Index 32

Pirate!

It's the year 1717, and you're in Charleston on the Carolina coast. My name is Jamie Flynn. There's a forest of ships tied up against the quay. Some have brought slaves from Africa. Others are loading up with deerskins for Europe.

But who are those shifty-looking men over there? Uh-oh! They've spotted me listening. They're coming this way! Agh, too late! Before I can struggle, they've put a sack over my head, and thrown me into a rowboat. 'Sharp eyes, eh? He's just what we need for a lookout!' Then it all goes black. I've been kidnapped by pirates!

Golden Age of Piracy

Between 1716 and 1726, pirate ships by the score roamed the seas near America and into the Caribbean. Many a lone vessel caught sight of a pirate ship racing towards them over the waves and knew they were doomed.

Historians now call it the Golden Age of Piracy. But for the victims of pirates it was anything but golden! Pirate leaders such as Black Bart, Black Sam Bellamy and Calico Jack were ruthless cut-throats, and you didn't want to be on a ship attacked by one of them!

Charleston

Florida

Gulf of Mexico

Cuba

Dominican Republic

Caribbean Sea

WARNING!

If you live in a seaport, you'd better watch out for 'press gangs' – ruthless gangs that recruit pirates by force!

A Pirate Ship

Oh no! It seems I've been taken aboard the most fearsome of all pirate ships, the *Queen Anne's Revenge*, flagship of the terrifying Blackbeard.

Like nearly all pirate ships, *Queen Anne's Revenge* is a stolen ship. To make it fast and dangerous, the pirates stripped away its cumbersome 'castles', the deck structures at front and back. Then they knocked through the lower decks to open it up so it could take lots of extra men. And they cut holes in the hull to poke 40 cannons through. That makes it a formidable ship for fast attack! Unarmed ships better watch out!

Blackbeard's ship

In 1996, divers found a wreck lying in 8.5 m (28 ft) of water just off Atlantic Beach in North Carolina. In 2011, the National Geographic Society confirmed that this was *Queen Anne's Revenge*, run aground in 1718, complete with its cannon. Among the thousands of items found was a medical syringe showing that Blackbeard did look after his crew!

North Carolina

Atlantic Ocean

Cutaway illustration of the
Queen Anne's Revenge

Beached!

It's hard to keep a pirate ship
in tip-top condition, because we
can't go into any regular port for
maintenance. We have to steal all the
equipment we need from the ships
we attack. And every now and then,
we need to run the ship aground to
scrape the hull clean of barnacles
and weeds that might slow us down.
That's seriously hard work!

Life on Board

'UP THE MAST, BOY! NOW!' That's the mate yelling! Because I'm small and light, and have sharp eyes, I'm the lookout in the crow's nest – the most dangerous place in the ship! It's the tiny bucket right up at the top of the main mast, swaying more than 15 m (50 ft) above the deck.

I often have to climb up slippery, wet rigging as gales are howling and waves crash over the ship. It's really, really frightening when the ship rolls over, the mast leans and I'm left hanging high out over the raging waves. I feel sick most of the time! The last lookout before me plunged to his death on the deck when his foot got caught by a stray sail line. But I can see a long way from up here – and if I'm the first to see a ship for us to attack, I'll get a reward of one gold piece!

Some of our crew were kidnapped like me, but many chose to come. Life is tough on other ships – and on land too, now. Being a pirate is dangerous, but you've got the freedom of the sea.

Below decks

Life on a pirate ship is no fun at all! The food's just stale biscuits and, if I'm lucky, a bit of salt beef so tough it'd be easier to eat my shoes (if I had any!). And there's no beds – just hammocks for the senior crew. Lookout boys like me just curl up on ropes or sacking below deck. It's really cold and wet and dark, and the smell is terrible. Ugh! AND there's RATS!

Blackbeard!

Oh no! I'm being hauled up before the Captain, the monstrous Blackbeard. His real name is Edward Teach, and he probably came from a decent Bristol family. But he's called Blackbeard because of his huge black beard. It's no ordinary beard, I can tell you! It's huge and dark and knotted into plaits that look like writhing snakes. And when he goes into battle, he often ties lighted fireworks into them to make himself look super scary! And now he's shouting at me like an angry bear!

They say Blackbeard is so strong he can cut a man in half with a single blow from his cutlass. And he's so nasty, he shot his own mate in the knees just for a laugh! But maybe he spreads these rumours himself. If his victims believe he's so dreadful, they'll give up without a fight when they hear Blackbeard is coming … I'm sure he just winked at me!

Kinds of pirate

The 'buccaneers' of the 1600s were pirates given 'letters of marque' by the French and British so they could legally raid Spanish enemy ships. A 'buccan' was the beach barbeque they liked. 'Privateers' were private ships hired by governments to attack enemies. 'Corsairs' were what the English called French pirates, and the French called Muslim pirates. 'Barbary pirates' were Muslim pirates from the Barbary Coast of North Africa.

Here's some other scary pirates:

Captain Kidd: Hanged 1701, London. Best prize: the *Quedagh Merchant*'s silks and gold

Black Bart Roberts: Killed 1722, off Nigeria. Best prize: 15 ships in three days!

Henry Morgan: Died 1688, Jamaica (in bed). Best prize: Destroying the Spanish fleet in Venezuela

Sam Bellamy: Died 1717 (in a storm). Best prize: *Whydah*'s indigo, gold and silver

Calico Jack Rackham: Hanged 1720, Jamaica. Crew included two women captured with him (right)

Anne Bonny & Mary Read: Escaped hanging because they were pregnant. Read died 1721. Bonny's end is uncertain

Walking the Plank!

Pirates look after each other well in a tight situation. But they're really brutal if anyone crosses them – and I mean BRUTAL!
It's amazing how many different ways they've found to punish those who rub a pirate crew up the wrong way! These are just some of the ways that pirates make anyone regret upsetting them …

Marooning: A deserter is left on a desert island with a gun and a bottle of rum. The rum is for courage to shoot himself – or he could just starve to death.

Keelhauling: This is a particularly nasty punishment. We tie the victim's hands and feet, and haul him right under the bottom of the boat (the keel).

Shooting: We can just shoot wrongdoers, but the cruellest pirates prolong the agony by shooting them in the knee. Then, they'll be crippled for life.

Walking the plank: Everyone thinks pirates make their enemies walk, blindfolded, off the end of a plank into the sea. But this is just a myth.

Dunking: If we don't want to kill a man, but just get him really worried, we'll string him up by his hands from the yard arm – the horizontal arm that holds the sails.

Flogging: The cat-o'-nine-tails is not a fluffy kitten – it's a particularly nasty whip made of nine ropes with knotted ends.

Clapping in irons: Of course, some victims are just locked in wrist and leg irons and thrown into the ship's hold.

The Pirate Code

Pirates may be lawless, but we have our rules! When anyone joins the crew, they must sign the Articles of Agreement – or else. The Articles are a list of rules on how to behave, how to divide up the loot and what compensation you get if you're badly injured.

Typical pirate rules:

1. Every man has a vote in what to do.

2. Every man has a share in booty.

3. No one is to play cards or dice for money.

4. Lights and candles must be out at 8 o'clock at night.

5. Pistols and cutlasses must be kept clean and fit for service.

6. No women are allowed on board.

7. Desertion in battle will be punished by death or marooning.

8. No one is to strike another on board, but all quarrels must be ended on shore, by sword and pistol.

9. If any man should lose a limb, he is to have 800 dollars.

10. The Captain and Quartermaster are to receive two shares of a prize; the master, boatswain, and gunner, one share and a half; and other officers one share and a quarter.

cutlass and Flintlock

Sometimes, ships surrender without a fight as soon as they see a pirate ship heading towards them. But if they don't, we may need to fight and overpower them. There's no passengers on a pirate ship – we all fight. So we all need weapons. Out at sea, we can't buy them from a shop, can we? So we have to steal them from the ships we attack – or we improvise. Some of the things we use weren't made as weapons.

WARNING!

If you see a small black ball that doesn't explode coming your way – you'd still better be careful. It might just be a stinkpot that sends out foul-smelling fumes.

Armed like a pirate... Your weapons must allow you to fight hand-to-hand in tight spaces between the rigging.

Cutlass: A pirate's favourite sword is short, but heavy enough to slash rope – or an arm.

Belaying pin: This is for securing ropes, but it's great for knocking your foe on the head!

Grappling hook: Chuck several over to your target ship, and yank it in close!

Sword: Some pirates choose a small sword for stabbing at the enemy, rather than a cutlass.

Flintlock: Blackbeard straps six to his waist ready to fire at the pull of a strip of silk.

Grenades: Light the fuse of these gunpowder-filled iron or clay balls, toss and... boom!

Boarding axe: Grab one to hack away at rigging – and your foe.

Marlin spike: Undo knots in the rigging with this, and use it as a dagger.

Caltrop or crowsfoot: Throw several on deck for cutting into feet.

Buckler: It may look like a small shield, but it's for punching and slashing.

Sneaky Tactics

'Ship ahoy!' I shout, as I spy a treasure ship sailing away in the distance. Blackbeard is cock-a-hoop – we haven't seen a ship for weeks and things were getting desperate. The chase is on! But it's not easy capturing a ship at sea. First you've got to get close. If it was heading this way, we could run up a false distress flag so the ship comes to help. The famous pirate Anne Bonny once got her crew to cover themselves in red paint and pretend to be dead after a battle! This tactic won't work for us, though, because our potential victims are sailing away from us.

We've caught up! But we want our prize in one piece. So first we fire a warning shot across its bows and tell it to heave to (stop). That's scary enough for most ships, I can tell you. But this one is not heaving to. Now we get serious! We pull alongside, so our cannons face it. Fire!!! We just want to slow it down, though. So we aim high above the hull and shoot away the rigging. The sails flap loose, and the ship drifts to a standstill...

Pirates made sure their ships were kept as light as possible. That way they could catch up with merchant ships slowed down by their cargo. Many pirates sailed in sloops, which were the fastest ships on the sea. Some could sail at over 11 knots (20 km/h or 12.6 mph).

Death is coming...

Pirates have such a fearsome reputation that sometimes we only have to run up our pirate flag to scare a ship into surrender. The flag is black and marked with a skull and crossbones! Some call it Captain Death. Others call it the Jolly Roger – but there's nothing jolly about it!

Stand by to Board!

Now we're pulling right alongside. Some men fling over grappling hooks and begin to yank the ships together. As we close in, men up in the rigging spray the deck with shot from blunderbuss rifles. The crew of the prize ship run for cover. Blackbeard yells, 'Stand by to board!' Oh yes, we're ready, armed to the teeth with stinkpots and grenades, spikes and pins, cutlasses and crowsfeet. Up above, men are already swinging across, cutlasses and axes in hand, to cut away the rigging for the attack. Here we go!

Not all targets were ships. In May 1718, Blackbeard anchored outside Charleston, captured some leading citizens and threatened to execute them unless the town paid him off with medical supplies. But the two pirates who rowed the messenger back to port got drunk for days. As Blackbeard was about to carry out his threat, a message at last got through from the drunken pirates. The town agreed his terms just in time and Blackbeard spared his captives.

Once the battle was won, we often set the crew of the prize ship free, if they were of no use to us. When Blackbeard took the *Concorde*, he forced the surgeons, carpenters, cooks and pilot to join him.

Booty Haul

Once we've captured our prize ship, it's time to divide the spoils. Of course, Blackbeard takes the lion's share, but we pirates like to share out our booty. Gold and jewels are nice. But most ships don't carry them. What we usually get is food, cloth, tools and weapons, which are far more use to us. You can't eat gold when you're hungry! And you can't buy weapons out at sea. Sugar, wine and tobacco are always nice treats after months on stale beer and dry salty biscuits.

Buried Treasure myth

Robert Louis Stevenson's famous story *Treasure Island* (1883) gave people the idea that pirates often buried their stolen treasure, then left maps with clues about where to find it. But only one pirate is known to have buried treasure – William Kidd. He hid his loot in 1701 when he thought he was going to be arrested. But he didn't leave a map...

Pieces of eight

A piece of eight was a Spanish silver coin. Pirates rarely saw them. But people often link them with pirates because in *Treasure Island*, Long John Silver's parrot keeps repeating 'Pieces of eight!'

Pirate Haunts

After bagging that last prize, we can have a holiday! So we're off to Port Royal in Jamaica. Back in 1657, Port Royal let pirates come ashore in return for their protection from the Spanish. Soon every pirate on the oceans was sailing in to drink, gamble and meet girls. It was so wild that people were soon calling it the wickedest city on Earth. Then, 25 years ago, Port Royal was overwhelmed by a devastating earthquake. It's just not the same now, they say. Still, I'm looking forward to getting my feet on dry land!

Even the local parrots and monkeys come to the inns and get drunk in Port Royal! They say that's where Blackbeard found his own pet monkey.

Disaster strikes

At 11.43 a.m. on 7th June 1692, an earthquake struck Port Royal. The city was utterly devastated, as buildings crumbled and sank into the sand. This disaster was followed by a tsunami that washed away half the city. Up to 3,000 people died at once and 2,000 more later, from disease. Most of the survivors moved to Kingston, which became the capital of Jamaica.

Dressed like a Pirate

My own clothes wore out long ago, so I've got a new suit of pirate garb. We pirates have our own way of dressing. It's a mix of items stolen from our victims – and ones made from the rolls of luxurious cloth we've rescued from a ship. Just like many of my fellows, I'm wearing a jacket that's way too big for me, and my pantaloons are baggy and colourful. But I look every inch a pirate.

Phrase book

Pirates have their own way of talking...

Shiver me timbers! Expressing a nasty shock, based on the way the timbers (masts) shiver (shake) when hit by a cannonball

Avast ye! Stop (you)!

Anchors aweigh! Lift the anchor just clear of the bottom

Landlubber A clumsy person, who is happiest living ashore. It's the worst insult to a pirate.

Strike colours! Lower the flag and surrender

Swabbie A swab is a kind of mop, and a swabbie is the poor idiot who has to scrub all the blood off the decks after a fight. Ugh! That's me after I ran into the first mate by accident...

Three-cornered hat!

My proudest possession is my three-cornered or tricorne hat. Ordinary crew aren't allowed to wear them, but I'm Blackbeard's boy now, so I've got one. Tricornes don't just look good. The broad brim keeps the spray off your face, and the turn-up acts like a gutter.

That's Your Lot

In November 1718, we were partying on Ocracoke Island off the Carolina coast when we saw two ships flying naval colours heading our way. With the tide out, they couldn't reach us over the sandbar that night. Next morning, as the tide rose and the naval ships raced in over the bar, Blackbeard calmly steered his ship towards the beach. He must have gone mad! But then he guided us through a tiny gap between the beach and a sandbar. The naval ships slammed into the bar and stuck. Aha! But as our ship fired its cannons at them, it lurched back and soon we were stuck, too.

It looked like all the naval sailors had been killed by our cannons, so we rowed across and boarded their ship. Oh no, it was a trap. They were faking! Their captain, Maynard, met Blackbeard face-to-face. They both fired pistols. But as Blackbeard swung his sword for the final blow, another sailor cut his throat from behind. That was the end of Blackbeard. And my life as a pirate! Hooray!

Many pirates who were caught alive were taken to London, tried and then hanged – including Captain Kidd. The rope broke when they tried to hang Kidd, so they had to hang him a second time.

Ten Pesky Pirate Facts

1 There were around 2,000 pirates in the Caribbean in 1717.

2 Pirates compensated men who were injured in battle. For example, a man who lost his right arm would receive 600 pieces of eight or six slaves (16 pieces of eight = one doubloon).

3 If someone betrayed a pirate crew, they were sent an ace of spades playing card. This meant they were going to die...

4 Some pirates really did have wooden legs. They often fought, and anyone badly wounded in the leg might need to have it cut off – to stop the gangrene (infection) spreading and killing him.

5 Pirates really did catch parrots in South America and teach them to talk. But they usually sold them later for a high price.

6 When Dutch pirate Dirk Chivers captured naval captain Sawbridge, the prisoner complained so much that Chivers sewed up his mouth with a needle and thread.

7 In 1825, when pirates captured the ship *Eliza Ann*, they hacked the crew to death. But they spared a woman called Lucretia Parker who lived to tell the tale.

8 Pirates liked to give their ships scary names. Benito de Soto called his the *Black Joke*. And Danish pirate John Derdrake's vessel had the ominous name, *Sudden Death*.

9 It was not uncommon for pirates to kidnap boys. Some boys, called 'powder monkeys', had to keep the cannons topped up with gunpowder. Their life was very tough indeed!

10 When Blackbeard was killed, they cut off his head and tossed his body over the side. It was said that his headless body still swam around, yelling, 'Where's my head?'

Glossary

Belaying pin

A solid metal or wooden handle used to secure rigging – and a handy weapon

Buccaneer

A pirate legalized by the British and French with 'letters of marque' to attack Spanish ships

Buckler

A small, round shield that can be used as an offensive weapon

Cutlass

A shortish, heavy hacking sword with one cutting edge, easy to wield

Doubloon

A Spanish gold coin used between 1537 and 1849 – pirate currency!

Flintlock

A pistol fired by striking a flint against metal to create the spark that sets fire to the powder

Keelhauling

Dragging someone under the bottom of the boat for punishment

Marooning

Leaving someone stranded on a desert island as a punishment

Swashbuckler

A daring adventurer – from someone who cheekily swashed (slapped) your buckler

Tricorne

A three-cornered hat popular with pirates

Scuttle

To sink your ship on purpose

INDEX

B
Barbary pirates 12
Blackbeard 8, 12–13, 20,
    21, 28–29, 30
booty 22–23
buccaneers 12
buried treasure 22

C
capturing ships 18–21, 30
catching pirates 28–29
clothes 26–27
corsairs 12
crow's nest 10
cutlasses 16

D
dunking 15

F
flags 19
flintlocks 16
flogging 15
food 10

G
Golden Age of Piracy 7

H
hanging of pirates 29

I
injuries 30

K
keelhauling 14
Kidd, Captain William 12,
    22, 29
kidnapping 6, 30

L
life on a pirate ship 10–11

M
marooning 14
medical supplies 20

N
names of ships 30

P
parrots 23, 24, 30
phrases 26
pieces of eight 23
Pirate Code, The 15
pirate rules 15
pirate ships 8–11, 30

pirates, famous 12–13
Port Royal, Jamaica
    24–25
'powder monkeys' 30
privateers 12
punishments 14–15, 30

Q
Queen Anne's Revenge
    8–9

R
running aground 9, 28

S
scary pirates 12–13
shooting 14

T
tactics 18–19, 28–29
three-cornered hats 27
treasure 22–23

W
walking the plank 14
weapons 16–17
wooden legs 30

The Author

John Farndon is Royal Literary Fellow at Anglia Ruskin University in Cambridge, UK, and the author of a huge number of books for adults and children on science and nature. He has been shortlisted four times for the Royal Society's Young People's Book Prize.

The Artist

Tatio Viana lives in Madrid, Spain, and worked as an art director before turning to what he really loves: illustrating. Entirely self-taught, he creates his artwork digitally, but dreams of illustrating his own stories with paints and crayons – especially for his son, Elías, to read.